Word Magic: Unleash your Imagination with Creative Writing for Kids

Mandy Mercy Gopal Karpagam

INDIA · SINGAPORE · MALAYSIA

ISBN 979-8-89026-367-4

CONTENTS

Ways to Say "Happy"..5

Ways to Say "Excited"..7

Ways to Say "Sad" or "Disappointed" 13

Ways to Say "Embarrassed"..21

Ways to Say "Angry"...25

Ways to Say "Afraid"...35

Ways to Say "Shocked"..45

Ways to Say "Proud"...57

Appendix..*61*

WAYS TO SAY "HAPPY"

Grinned from Ear to Ear like a Cheshire Cat

Beamed with Delight

Flashed a Megawatt Smile

A Huge Smile Spread Across the Face

WAYS TO SAY "EXCITED"

Chirped Merrily and Enthusiastically

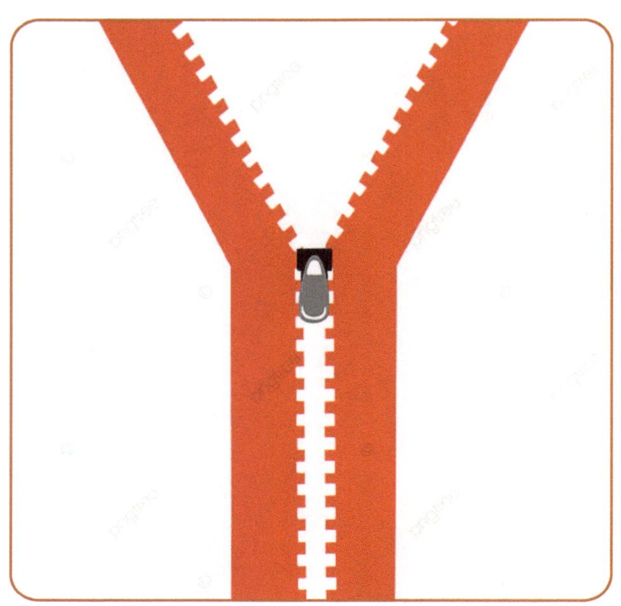

With Energy Zipping Through the Veins

The Eyes Lit up in Excitement

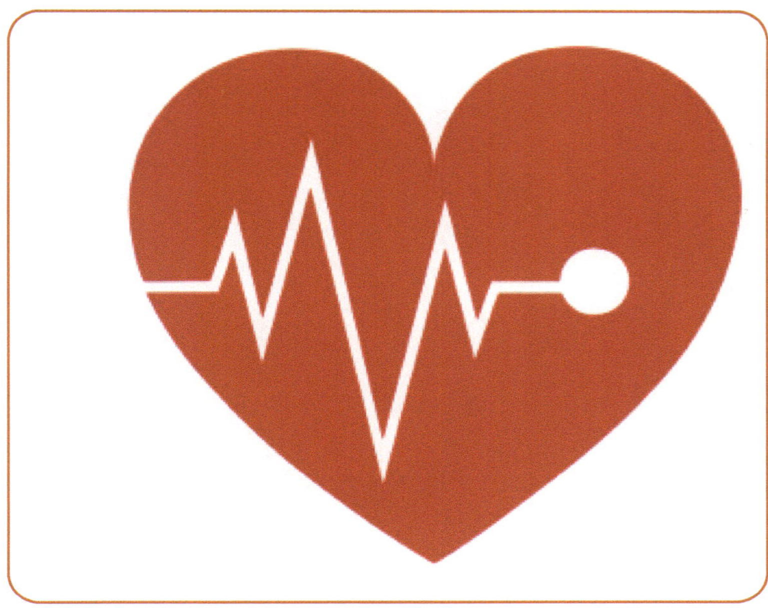

With The Heart Pumping In Excitement

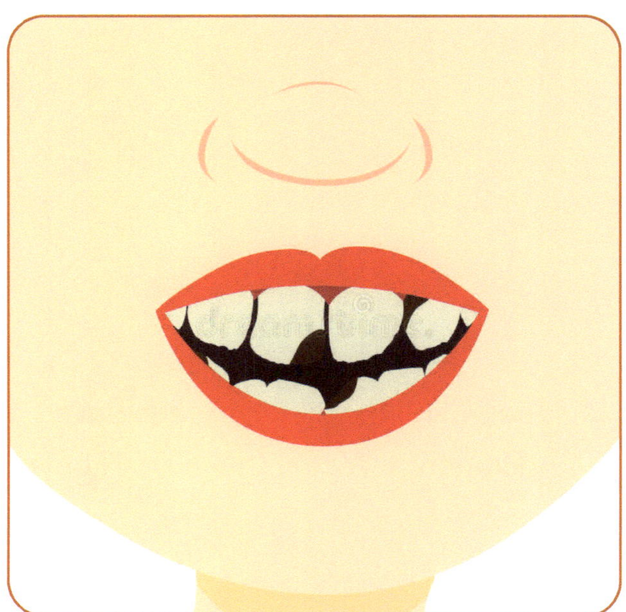

Broke Out in Excited Squeals

Felt a Surge of Excitement

Eyes Glinted and Heartbeat Raced as
Though it Was a Car on a Highway

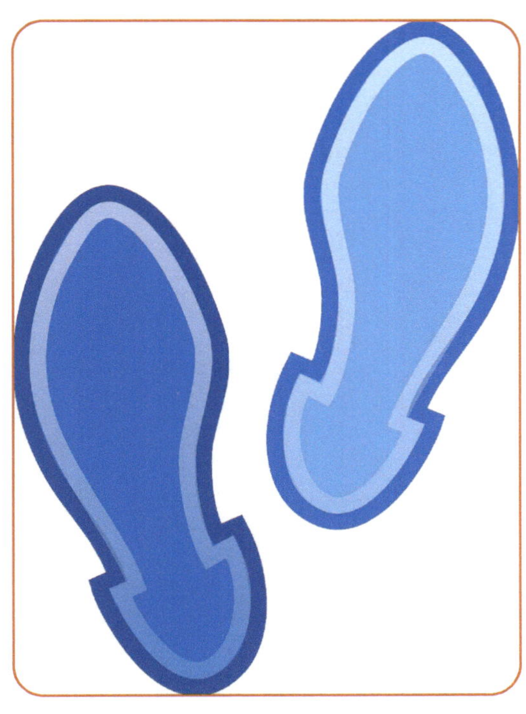

Walked With a Spring in
Every Step

WAYS TO SAY "SAD" OR "DISAPPOINTED"

Whimpering Softly

Groaning in Dismay

Appeared Crestfallen

Wailing Pitiably

Seemed Distraught

Heart Sank Like it Weighed a
Tonne of Bricks

Wallowed in his Sorrow

Cried in Despair

Sobbed Silently

Tears Welled Up in the Eyes

Wiped Tears Off his Face

Heart Shattered Into a Million Tiny Pieces

Looked Devastated by the News

On the Verge of Tears

WAYS TO SAY "EMBARRASSED"

Cheeks Turned a Deep Shade of Crimson Red

Hung the Head Low in Mortification

Apologised Profusely

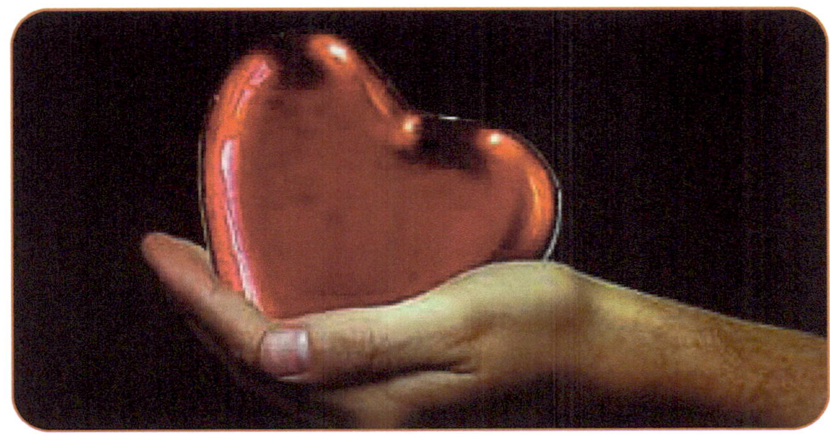

Felt so Humiliated that Shame and
Embarrassment Gripped the Heart

Wished that the Earth would
Swallow Me up that Instant

WAYS TO SAY "ANGRY"

Stared Daggers at

The Face Radiated Heat Like a Hot Pan and You Could have Cooked a Three-Course Meal on it

Roared in Rage

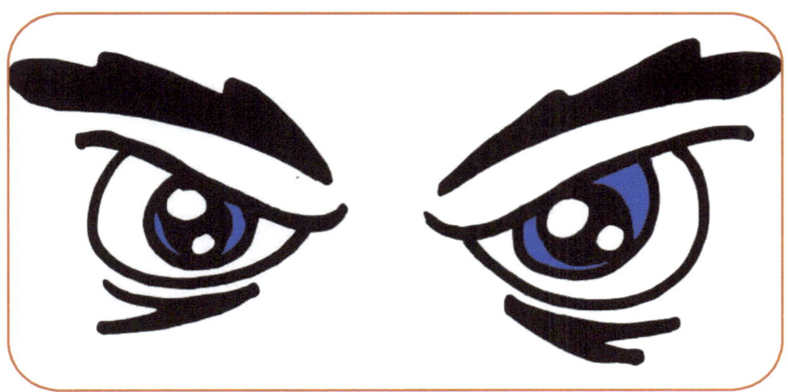

Gaze Blazed with Fury

Stormed Off in Anger

Gave a Tongue-Lashing

Reprimanded

Chided

Lashed at

Raised the Clenched Fist in the Air

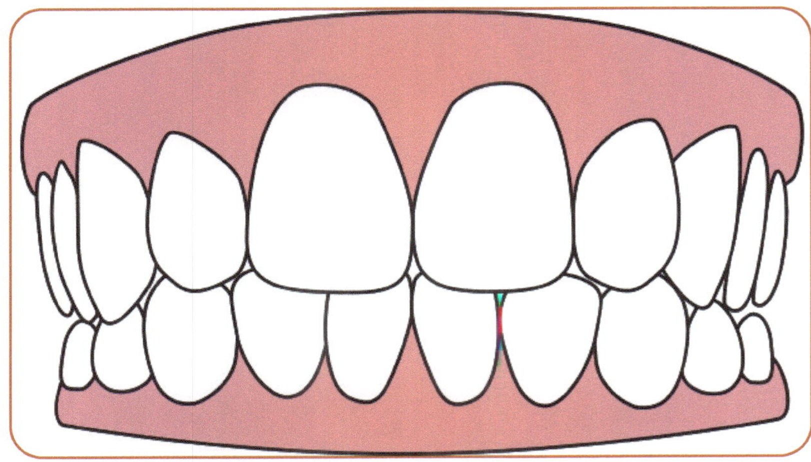

Gritted the Teeth in Anger

Sneered Angrily

Retaliate in Fuming Anger

Completely Overwhelmed/
Consumed By Rage

Face Reddened in Rage

Warned Sternly

Glared Fiercely at

Infuriated by the Scene/Person

WAYS TO SAY "AFRAID"

Something Inside Quivered with Nervousness

Watched in Horror as

Terror Filled the Body

With Dread on the Face

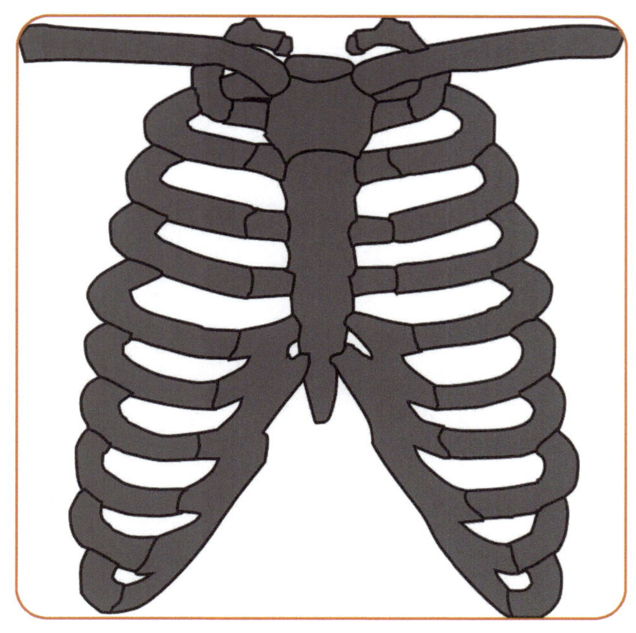

Heart Palpitated/Pounded Loudly
Like African Drums against the
Ribcage/Chest

Beads of Perspiration Dripped
from the Forehead/Temples

Entire Body Shook in Trepidation

Could Not Muster Up Enough
Courage to do

Terrified Beyond Words

Butterflies Fluttered Up a Storm
Inside My Stomach

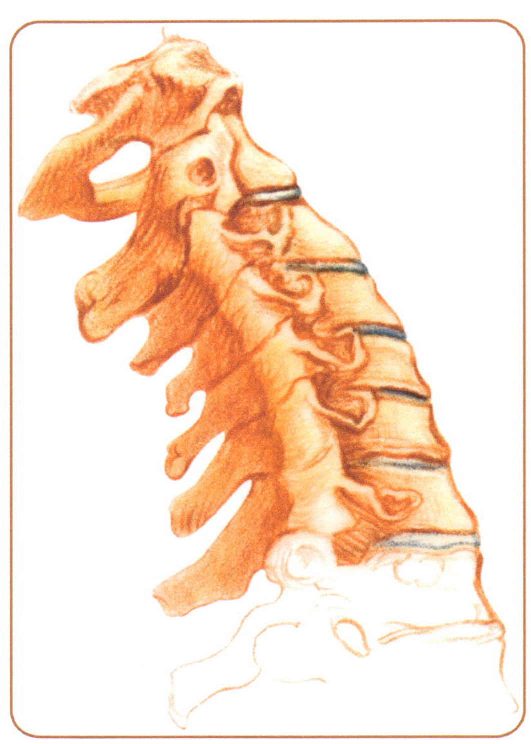

A Chill Ran Down the Spine

Confidence Waning as
She Stared at it

Trembling Like a Leaf in a Strong
Gust of Wind

Shrieked in Fright/The Face Turned
as White/As Pale as a Ghost

Fear Reflected in the Eyes

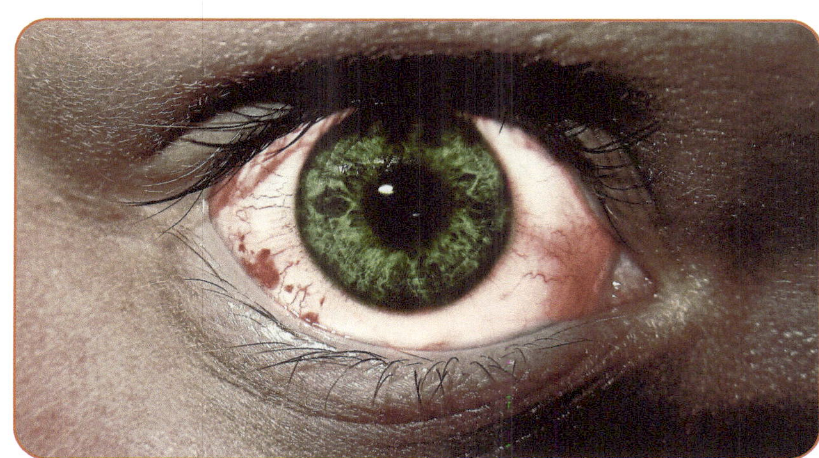

Was Petrified by the

Paralysed in Fear

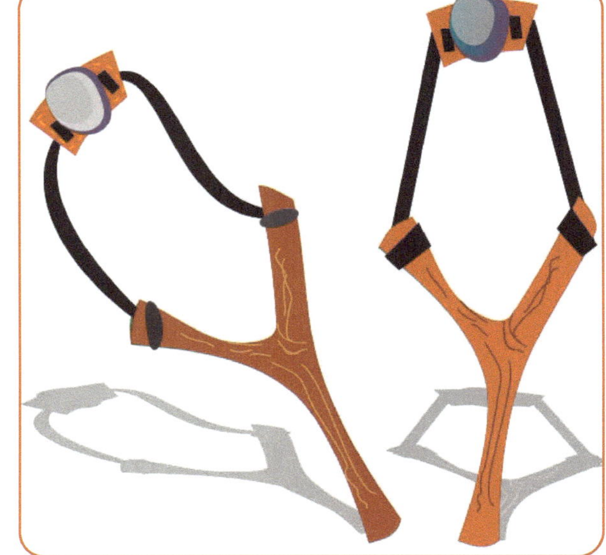

Catapulted Him/Her into a
State of Frantic Frenzy

WAYS TO SAY "SHOCKED"

Breathing was Rapid and Shallow

Stood Rooted to the Ground Like
a Statue, Transfixed by the Scene

Not Knowing What to Do/How to
React to the Situation

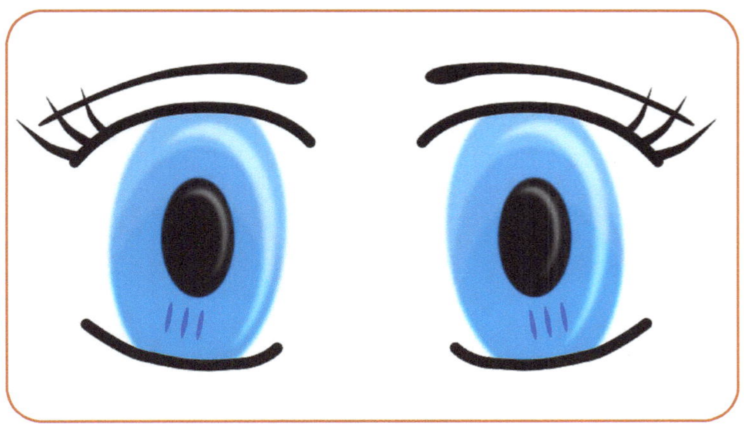

Eyes Grew Twice their Size

Sweat Trickled Down the Neck

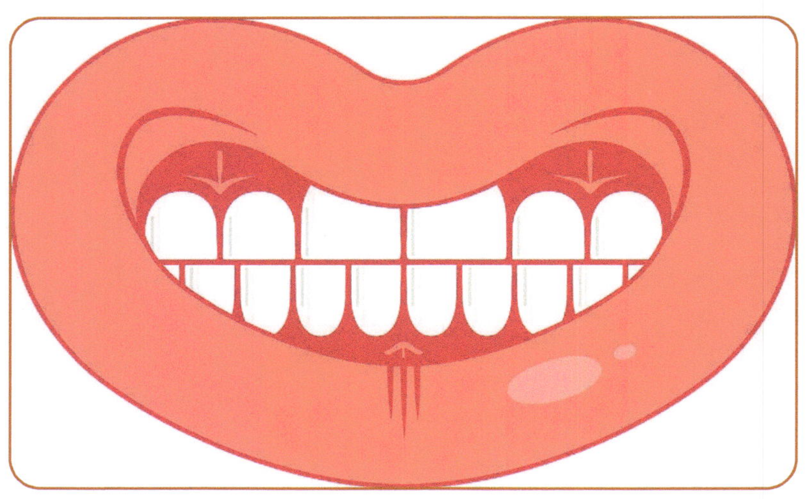

Heart was in the Mouth

Mouth Fell Agape in
Astonishment/Jaw Dropped Open
in Shock

Froze in Shock

Eyes Widened in Disbelief/
Incredulity

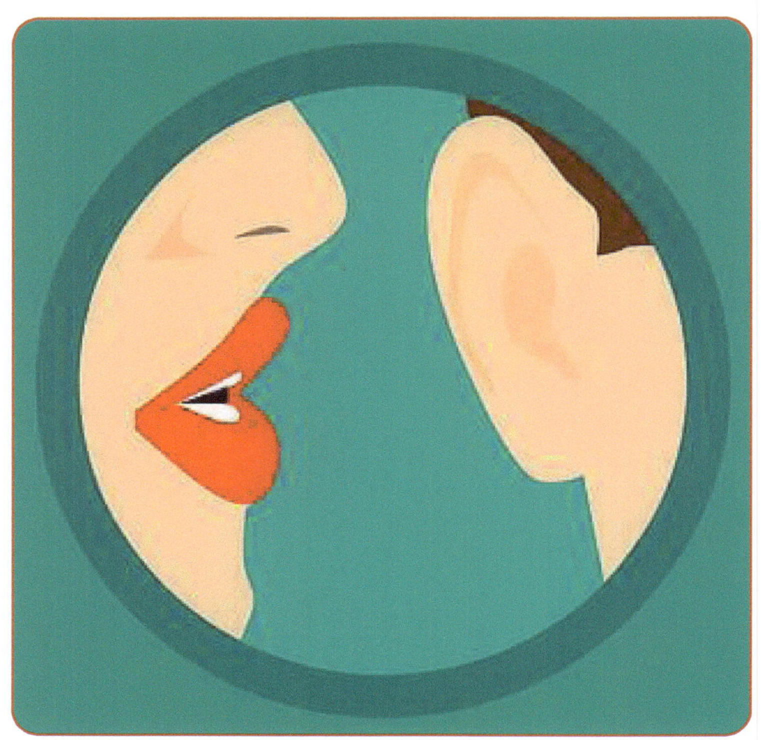

An Ear-Piercing Scream Escaped
from the Mouth

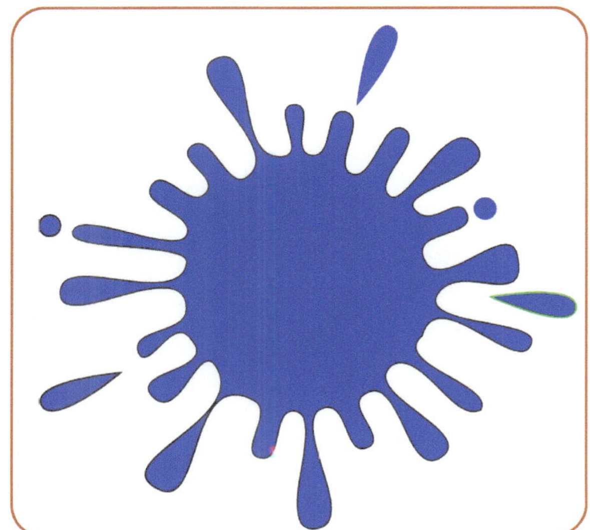

Out of the Blue

A Sudden/Abrupt Pat on the Back
Jolted Him/Her Back to Attention

Snapped Back to the Present

Mind was a Whirlpool of Hazy Thoughts

Looked Panic-Stricken

Felt a Sinking Feeling in the Pit of the Stomach

Flooded with Sudden Shock

Was Dumbfounded/Dumbstruck

Shaking Myself Out of the Initial State of Shock, I Took a Deep Breath

Gasped in Horror and Panted for
Breath Like a Fish Out of Water

At the Sight of the Sudden Scare

WAYS TO SAY "PROUD"

Stood Tall and Erect

With My Shoulders Arched Back

Gave Myself a Pat on the Back

I Felt a Sudden Burst of
Pride and Bliss

Beamed with Pride and was
Delighted/Whooped with Joy/
Raised my Clenched Fist in the
Air/Pumped My Fist Up in the Air
Joyfully

They Lavished Praise on Him/Her

APPENDIX

Ways to say...

SAID	SHOUT	WALK	RUN	GOOD	ATE	DRANK	YUMMY
UTTERED/ RETORTED/ ORDERED	HOLLERED/ SNARLED	STROLLED	ZOOMED/ HURRIED	GREAT /SPECTACULAR/ AMAZING	GOBBLED DOWN	SLURPED	MOUTH-WATERING
REMARKED /MURMURED/ ASKED	BELLOWED	TRUDGED/ STAGGERED	DASHED	FANTASTIC	DEVOURED	SIPPED ON	TASTY
MUTTERED /MUMBLED/ GRUMBLED	SHRIEKED/	HOBBLED	RUSHED	IMPRESSIVE/ UNBELIEVABLE	DUG IN RAVENOUSLY	GULPED DOWN	SCRUMPTIOUS
CHIRPED/ ANNOUNCED	SCREAMED	LIMPED	RACED/ SPRINTED	SUPERB	WOLFED DOWN		SUMPTUOUS
COMPLAINED/ WHINED/ SIGHED/ SNAPPED	YELLED	AMBLED/ TIPTOED/ LOITERED	SPED /SCURRIED/ STORMED OFF	APT	MUNCHED ON		DELICIOUS
WHISPERED/ THREATENED/ BLACKMAILED	BARKED/ THREATENED	SAUNTERED/ MARCHED	CHARGED/ BOLTED	WONDERFUL	SNACKED ON		DELECTABLE

SAID	SHOUT	WALK	RUN	GOOD	ATE	DRANK	YUMMY
COMMENTED/ HISSED/ WHEEZED/ CACKLED/ STAMMERED/ CROAKED/ INTERRUPTED /IMPLORED /BEGGED/ PLEADED/ REQUESTED /INSTRUCTED/ COMMANDED	EXCLAIMED /CRIED/ REPLIED	JOGGED/ STRODE AWAY	DARTED/ CHASED/ PURSUED/ FLED FROM THE SCENE/ ESCAPED/ ABSCONDED/ BEAT A HASTY RETREAT	MAGNIFICENT	NIBBLED ON		SAVOURY